AF843658

The Economics of Occupational Safety and Health

The Economics of Occupational Safety and Health

John Ruser

U.S. Bureau of Labor Statistics
ruser.john@bls.gov

Richard Butler

Brigham Young University
USA
richard_butler@byu.edu

now
the essence of knowledge

Boston – Delft

Foundations and Trends® in Microeconomics

Published, sold and distributed by:
now Publishers Inc.
PO Box 1024
Hanover, MA 02339
USA
Tel. +1-781-985-4510
www.nowpublishers.com
sales@nowpublishers.com

Outside North America:
now Publishers Inc.
PO Box 179
2600 AD Delft
The Netherlands
Tel. +31-6-51115274

The preferred citation for this publication is J. Ruser and R. Butler, The Economics of Occupational Safety and Health, Foundations and Trends® in Microeconomics, vol 5, no 5, pp 301–354, 2009

ISBN: 978-1-60198-382-4

Foundations and Trends® in Microeconomics
Volume 5 Issue 5, 2009

Editorial Scope

Foundations and Trends® in Microeconomics will publish survey and tutorial articles in the following topics:

- Environmental Economics
- Contingent Valuation
- Environmental Health Risks
- Climate Change
- Endangered Species
- Market-based Policy Instruments
- Health Economics
- Moral Hazard
- Medical Care Markets
- Medical Malpractice
- Insurance economics
- Industrial Organization
- Theory of the Firm
- Regulatory Economics
- Market Structure
- Auctions
- Monopolies and Antitrust
- Transaction Cost Economics
- Labor Economics
- Labor Supply
- Labor Demand
- Labor Market Institutions
- Search Theory
- Wage Structure
- Income Distribution
- Race and Gender
- Law and Economics
- Models of Litigation
- Crime
- Torts, Contracts and Property
- Constitutional Law
- Public Economics
- Public Goods
- Environmental Taxation
- Social Insurance
- Public Finance
- International Taxation

Information for Librarians

Foundations and Trends® in Microeconomics, 2009, Volume 5, 8 issues. ISSN paper version 1547-9846. ISSN online version 1547-9854. Also available as a combined paper and online subscription.

Foundations and Trends® in
Microeconomics
Vol. 5, No. 5 (2009) 301–354

DOI: 10.1561/0700000036

The Economics of Occupational Safety and Health

John Ruser[1,*] and Richard Butler[2]

[1] *U.S. Bureau of Labor Statistics, ruser.john@bls.gov*
[2] *Brigham Young University, USA, richard_butler@byu.edu*

Abstract

Economic incentives play an important role in occupational safety and health, affecting the behavior and decisions of workers, firms and government. This monograph discusses factors that affect workers' decisions about whether to choose risky jobs, how careful to be on the job, and how long to remain off work during recovery from injury. The monograph also examines occupational risk-related costs that influence the following safety decisions of a firm: wage premiums paid to attract workers to risky jobs, premiums for workers' compensation insurance, government fines for safety violations, and injury-related costs such as workplace disruptions and loss of worker specific job skills. This monograph also considers the influence of government, focusing on the enactment and enforcement of safety and health standards and the safety incentives of workers' compensation insurance systems. We find broad consensus in the empirical literature that workers and firms respond to economic incentives in making safety decisions. Economic incentives play an important role in occupational risk prevention. Sometimes these incentives improve safety; but, in other cases they have an adverse effect on safety.

[*] The views expressed in this monograph represent the views of the author and do not necessarily represent the views of the Bureau of Labor Statistics or the U.S. Department of Labor.

Contents

1

Introduction

Occupational injuries are random events, affected by the activities of workers, firms, and government. The safety efforts of workers and firms respond to a variety of economic incentives, and these incentives can be altered by government. Together, the analysis of these incentives and their outcomes forms the economics of occupational safety and health.

The occupational safety and health literature discusses factors that affect workers' decisions about whether to choose risky jobs, how careful to be on the job, and how long to remain off work during recovery from injury or illness. These factors influencing worker decisions include the wage–risk premium, pain and suffering from injuries, and income benefits paid during out-of-work recovery periods.

This monograph examines occupational risk-related costs that influence the following safety decisions of a firm: wage premiums paid to attract workers to risky jobs, insurance payments to injured workers including sick leave and workers' compensation benefits, premiums for workers' compensation insurance, government fines for safety violations, and injury-related costs such as workplace disruptions and loss of worker-specific job skills. The small literature on workplace committees and employee financial involvement with the firm's profitability on accident outcomes is also reviewed.

This monograph also discusses the influence of government, focusing on the regulation of occupational risk through the enactment and enforcement of safety and health standards and the safety mandates of workers' compensation insurance systems. This monograph does not discuss the psychological literature on information processing, some of which suggests that workers may underestimate the severity of hazards in some occupations (see Pouliakas and Thoedossiou, 2010), nor does it address potential externalities associated with workplace injuries accruing to the families of those injured. Unfortunately, there is scant empirical literature on the latter topic.

We find broad consensus in the empirical literature that workers and firms respond to economic incentives in making safety decisions. Economic incentives play an important role in occupational risk prevention. Sometimes these incentives improve safety, but in other cases they have an adverse effect on safety.

The monograph reviews the theory of compensating differentials in Section 2 in which workers with varying tolerances for risk are matched with firms with alternative production (and hence, risk prevention) technologies. This theory suggests that wages increase with more job risk, other things equal. In Section 3, we discuss incentives created by the workers' compensation insurance system, both for workers and for firms. Next, in Section 4, the monograph discusses the modest impact of government safety inspections in the USA and Canada. Last, in Section 5, we close with some final observations on the impact of the business cycle and long-term effects on occupational health and safety.

2

Compensating Wage Differentials

The Scottish economist Adam Smith (1776) wrote "The wages of labour vary with the ease or hardship, the cleanliness or dirtiness, the honourableness or dishonourableness of the employment."[1] This famous quotation succinctly summarizes the theory of compensating wage differentials.

Consider a simple example with two jobs (job 1 and job 2), which are identical except that job 2 has a higher risk of death than job 1. Fully informed workers will only work at job 2 provided they receive a greater wage than at job 1. The difference in wages — wage at job 2 minus wage at job 1 — is the compensating wage differential, because the higher wage compensates for the higher risk of death.

The theory of compensating wage differentials has evolved into a complex theory regarding the decisions of workers to select different jobs and of firms to select different technologies.[2] The theory assumes that workers differ in their concern about job risks (that is, they differ

[1] Wealth of Nations (1776) Book I, Chapter X, Part 1.

[2] The classic monograph on this topic is Rosen (1974); for a recent review of the literature, and formal discussion of these models allowing for socio-demographic differences (such as age), see Viscusi (1983), Aldy and Viscusi (2007), Kniesner and Leeth (2009).

in their willingness to work in a risky environment, i.e., they differ in their "risk aversion"). While most workers prefer safer jobs, some workers are more willing to face more risk for a variety of economic, demographic, and taste reasons. The theory predicts that these less risk-averse workers require smaller compensating wage differentials to work at riskier jobs than the more risk-averse workers. The theory also predicts that less risk-averse workers will choose to work at riskier jobs than the more risk-averse workers. In Figure 2.1, these less risk-averse workers sort themselves toward the right of the market wage–risk equilibrium curve (or locus of wage/risk pairs offered in the market). Thus, workers tend to sort among different jobs according to their preference for risk.

Firms produce safety and output, and as technology differs across firms, the costs of delivering a safe workplace also vary. If the firm does not invest in safety, then it must pay a higher wage than if it does invest in safety. The firm must choose either to pay a higher compensating wage to workers, or provide more safety, depending on whether the wages it saves over time exceed the costs of the new safety equipment. Hence, the theory of compensating differentials predicts that firms with higher safety costs will be less likely to invest in safety and thus will have higher accident rates and pay higher wages.

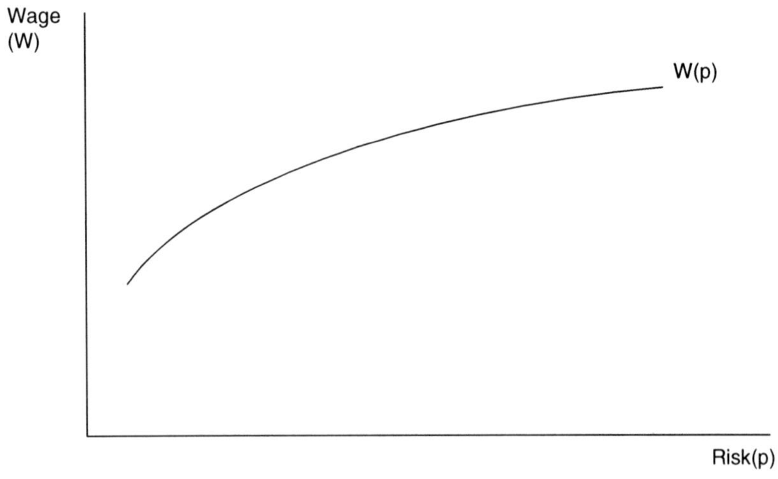

Fig. 2.1 Relationship between wage and job risk for a hypothetical job.

The result is market equilibrium where different levels of job risk are associated with different levels of wages. This market equilibrium in Figure 2.1 shows the equilibrium wage–risk curve as an upward sloping line, consistent with the theory of compensating differentials.

2.1 Estimating Wage–risk Trade-offs

This compensating wage–risk curve plays a key role in the economics of occupational risk prevention (ORP). The implications of the theory of compensating wage differentials for ORP are that workers and firms choose different levels of risk in response to wage differences. However, there is very little work that actually focuses on how these incentives directly affect occupational risk choice.

Previous research has focused on estimating wage–risk trade-offs. In looking across different jobs, the theory predicts that there is a positive relationship between job risk and wages, and that such wage premiums for risk will tend to fall as workers age (Aldy and Viscusi, 2007). Of course, other factors also affect the level of wages besides job risk, necessitating multivariate statistical analyses to hold constant other factors that might influence wages. These analyses typically utilize data on individual workers' wages and the injury and fatality rates associated with their industries or occupations. Wages are regressed on worker, firm, and job characteristics, including injury and fatality rates, with the estimated coefficient on the risk variable indicating how much observed wages change with unit changes in job risk.

For example, a given regression analysis might find that annual wages increase \$50 with an increase in the fatality rate of 1 death per 100,000 workers. For fatal risk, the change in wages is typically expressed in terms of the "value of a statistical life" (VSL). Suppose, to continue our example, that a statistical analysis determines that a worker receives \$50 annually for an increase in the annual risk of death of one worker in 100,000. If one worker would give up \$50 for a similar reduction in fatality risk, then 100,000 workers will collectively give up \$5,000,000. Among these 100,000 workers, a drop in the fatality risk of 1 in 100,000 results in one fewer death. Collectively, workers are willing to give up \$5 million for that one fewer death; so the VSL is \$5 million.

Economists express wage–risk trade-offs in terms of VSL to help inform public policy decisions: VSL indicates the amount that society is willing to pay to avoid the loss of a statistical life. This measures the societal benefit from saving a statistical life. In deciding whether a particular government safety standard passes a cost–benefit test, the VSL can be balanced against costs of saving a statistical life (reducing the probably of death). Hence, this helps inform decisions about which safety standards should be adopted in a world with limited resources.

VSL measures the implicit amount that society is willing to pay to reduce the occurrence of one anonymous death, but this differs from the value of a real life — i.e., the case of specific life-saving situation. For example, society might be willing to spend more to extract a specific miner trapped in a collapsed tunnel than would be predicted by the VSL.

2.2 Empirical Estimates of the Value of a Statistical Life

Most recent analyses on the value of a statistical life (VSL) come from US labor market data (particularly studies conducted before 1990), though more recent research extends such analyses to labor markets in other countries. Perhaps the most inclusive survey of this literature is Viscusi and Aldy (2003), who report USA labor markets typically show VSLs in the fairly wide range of $4 million to $9 million. Studies of Canadian labor markets typically show VSLs in the range of $3–$6 million. According to Viscusi and Aldy (2003), studies of other countries tend to be broadly consistent with the estimates in the USA and Canada, though international estimates tend to be somewhat lower for reasons explained below.

The wide range of VSL estimates might be due to different data sets and different estimation methodologies, as well as the different VSLs between international workers and their North American counterparts. More recent research examines factors that lead to these differences, focusing on income, gender, age, union status, and other institutional features of the labor market.

Income. Economists postulate that safety is a normal good, so that people demand more safety as income increases (Viscusi, 1978). Viscusi and Aldy find that developing countries tend to have lower VSLs than do developed countries. This is consistent with lower income levels in developing countries. Conducting a meta-analysis of studies of the relationship between income and VSL, Viscusi and Aldy concluded that a 10 percent increase in income increases VSL by 5–6 percent.

Age. Worker demographic characteristics may affect risk aversion, the demand for safety and hence the observed wage–risk trade-off. Age is one of the demographic factors that might be important. It would seem that as a person ages, he/she would attach a lower value of life, and Viscusi and Aldy (2003) and Aldy and Viscusi (2007) found that "numerous analyses have shown that the VSL is a decreasing function of age." For example, Rosen (1988) estimated that a 48-year-old person has a VSL that is 10 percent less than that of a 36-year-old person.

Recent research (Kniesner et al., 2006), however, suggested that the VSL may have an inverted U-shape with age, meaning that the VSL first increases with age until the worker is about 50 years old, and then decreases after that age. The VSL for a 50 year old was roughly 2.5 times as great as the VSL for a worker of age 18–21. Even though the VSL declined with age for those over 50, it was still over 2 times as great for workers of age 57–65 than for workers of age 18–21. The innovation of Kniesner et al. (2006) was accounting for the connection between the VSL and consumption of goods. VSL rises with consumption, while consumption rises and then falls over the life cycle.

Gender. Gender may also affect VSLs due to gender differences in risk aversion. There have only been a very few US studies of this source of variation in VSLs, owing to the lack of published gender-specific injury and fatality rates. Leeth and Ruser (2003) reported that, overall, men but not women earned a pay premium for bearing additional workplace fatality risk. This gender disparity largely occurred because of the occupational distribution of workers. When the statistical analysis was separated by occupational category, the researchers found both men and women earning a compensating wage differential for fatal injury risk in blue-collar jobs, but also found neither men nor women earning a wage differential in white-collar jobs. The overall weak results for women reflect the fact that women tend to be found in relatively white-collar jobs. The weak VSL results for white-collar jobs may reflect the low level of fatality risk in these jobs, coupled with relatively low variation in risk across jobs, making it difficult for the statistical analysis to discern results for white-collar workers.

Unions. Unions may affect VSLs in at least three ways. First, unions may bargain on behalf of workers for workplace safety in addition to wages and benefits, effectively placing a greater value on safety improvements. Second, incentives to negotiate for safety by an individual worker will be lower than the incentives to negotiate for a union provided that the union is able to overcome the "free rider" problem: individuals who don't participate in the negotiation can "free ride" on the efforts of the negotiators on behalf of others. Union bargaining could mean higher demand for safety, resulting in greater compensating wage differentials for risk. Third, if workers underestimate job risk, they will not demand sufficient wage premiums. Unions may be able to provide information about job risks that is not available to non-union workers, or negotiate for information to be adequately provided to workers.

The empirical literature from the US labor market strongly supports these hypotheses. Nine of ten studies reviewed by Viscusi and Aldy (2003) found higher wage–risk premiums for union workers than for non-union workers. In fact, several of these studies failed to find a compensating differential for risk for non-union workers. Interestingly, the research on labor markets from other countries does not provide such strong findings. The results were mixed in studies of labor markets in the United Kingdom, Canada, India, and South Korea. Kniesner and Leeth (1991) did find higher VSLs in Australia than in the USA, a result they attributed to the higher rate of unionization in Australia.

Labor market features. Kniesner and Leeth (1991) hypothesized that the wide variation in estimated VSLs might reflect different aspects of the labor markets of different countries. One feature is the extent of unionization, whose influence was described above. Another influence is the strength of attachment of workers to firms. As compared to the USA, the Japanese labor market is characterized by long-term attachment of workers to firms and low worker mobility between firms. Low mobility, including a lack of worker sorting between jobs of different risk, may result in the absence of compensating wage differentials.

Consistent with this hypothesis, Kniesner and Leeth (1991) found no evidence in Japan of compensating wage differentials for job fatalities.

2.3 Empirical Estimates of Compensating Wage Differentials for Non-fatal Risk

Some research examines the wage premiums associated with higher risk of non-fatal injury. The additional difficulty facing these non-fatal risk analyses is that non-fatal injuries can vary greatly in nature and in severity. In the USA, for example, studies have differed in whether the injury included only injuries that resulted in lost workdays or all injuries recorded on government forms (including many that involved no lost workdays).

Viscusi and Aldy (2003) reported on 31 studies of the USA labor market and 8 studies from outside the USA that found statistically significant relationships between non-fatal injuries and wages. The estimated implicit values of a statistical injury varied widely in these studies, reflecting both differences in the estimating methodology and differences in the risk measures that were used. Viscusi and Aldy concluded that most USA studies have estimates in the range of $20,000–$70,000 per injury. In an updated analysis using 1998 data on job illnesses and wages, Wei (2007) finds wage differentials for one job-related illness episode per year ranges from 27 to 140 percent of annual earnings.

According to the theory of compensating differentials, different workers attach different values to life and injury, with the less risk-averse workers attaching lower VSL values. Some research sought to identify people with weaker risk aversion as indicated by non-work activities. For instance, one might presume that a smoker or a person who does not wear a seatbelt is less risk averse than a non-smoker or a seatbelt wearer. The former people would require smaller wage premiums to work at risky jobs. In fact, several studies, including Viscusi and Hersch (2001), found that smokers have lower wage premiums than do non-smokers. Hersch and Pickton (1995) found the implicit value of a lost-workday injury was twice as high for non-smokers who wore seatbelts as for smokers who did not wear seatbelts.

As with fatality risk, compensating wage differentials for non-fatal risk seems to vary with worker demographics. Leeth and Ruser (2003) found gender to be important in the wage–risk tradeoff: both men and women earned compensating wage differentials for non-fatal injury risk, but wage compensation was over three times larger for women than men. Consistent with this pattern, Hersch (1998) found strong evidence of compensating differentials for women (value of injury estimates ranging from $23,800 to $35,200), but surprisingly, none for men.

2.4 Criticisms of the Compensating Differentials Literature

While most economists accept the compensating differential model, some are skeptical of the results and either question the reliability of the statistical methodology or point to possible biases in the estimates.

One critique concerns the rationality assumption underlying worker choice (Leigh, 1991; Dorman, 1996). The simplest form of the theory and the empirical results assume that workers are fully informed and rational, at least for the "marginal, willing and able to change job" individual. However, if these marginal workers underestimate job risks (Knostantinos and Theodossiou, 2010), then they will not demand sufficiently large wage premiums for risk and VSLs will be too low. Leigh (1991) cited studies showing that workers, particularly younger workers, underestimate their risk from motor vehicle crashes. However, finding most younger workers underestimate risk is not sufficient to preclude compensating differentials in the labor market if those at the "margin" do correctly value risk.

In addition to underestimating risk, irrational workers may be overconfident about their ability to avoid risk; they may make errors in ranking jobs with different risk, and, as a result, improperly process information.[3]

[3] To the extent that workers' perceptions of risk differ from reality, then the study of compensating differentials can be improved by utilizing perceived risk values. Gegax et al. (1991) estimated compensating wage differentials using perceived workplace death rates directly collected from workers in a survey. They found wage–risk trade-offs for union and blue-collar workers, though these estimates were lower than comparable ones obtained using industry fatality rates. They also did not find statistically significant results for white-collar and non-unionized workers.

Additional criticisms of statistical methodology have the opposite implications for the VSL bias. First, the risk measures that are matched to data on individual workers are the risks also faced by groups of workers (usually by industry). The risk measures do not necessarily accurately measure the risks faced by each worker in the data, even when they measure the appropriate average level of risk. The resulting "errors in variables" measurement problem — of using average, aggregate, risk instead of worker-specific risk — leads to a downward bias in the estimated wage–risk trade-off.

Second, some believe that the measured compensating wage differentials do not reflect true wage–risk trade-offs. Instead these critics argue that risk measures are correlated with other job characteristics; therefore, the measured wage differentials actually reflect other unmeasured inter-industry differentials (Leigh, 1995; Dorman and Hagstrom, 1998). Dorman and Hagstrom (1998) argued that non-competitive elements of the US labor market are sufficiently strong to overcome the market mechanisms generating compensating differentials.

The problem with this criticism is that many compensating differential studies control for unmeasured effects of industry and occupation and still find differentials. For example, Leeth and Ruser (2003) frequently obtained statistically significant wage differentials even after controlling for both industry and occupation.

3

Incentive Effects of Workers' Compensation Insurance

3.1 Workers' Compensation — Institutional Details[1]

Workers' compensation (WC) insurance in the USA is legislated by individual state laws (and a Federal law to cover Federal employees). However, the institutional characteristics of workers' compensation are broadly consistent across states and similar to many systems outside the USA. Hence, the implications of the USA workers' compensation system for occupational risk prevention will carry over to other countries.

These laws make employers liable for all medical expenses and a portion of lost wages of an injured worker. The laws also provide for rehabilitation services and the payment of income benefits to dependents in the case of a workplace fatality. The employer is generally liable to pay these benefits for any injury arising out of and in the course of employment, regardless of who is at fault.[2] The liability imposed on the employer is exclusive: the injured worker cannot sue for additional compensation.

[1] The text in this section draws heavily from Ruser (1985).

[2] However, states have instituted certain exclusions, such as the case where the worker is under the influence of alcohol or drugs.

Some large firms and groups of smaller firms are able to self-insure their liabilities. Generally, however, employers are required to purchase insurance to cover their potential liabilities. In five states, the insurance for those not self-insuring is provided by monopoly state funds. The remaining 45 states provide that insurance be purchased from a private insurance carrier or, in 20 states, from a state fund that competes with the private carriers. The procedures for calculating insurance premiums are similar across states.

In calculating premiums, the firm's workers are placed into one or more of approximately 600 industrial–occupational classifications. On the basis of these classifications, the firm is assigned "manual rates" which are premium rates reflecting the average loss conditions found in each classification. "Manual premiums" are then calculated by multiplying the manual rate by the payroll of workers in the classification. These manual premiums are summed for all classifications to arrive at the manual premium for the firm.

The actual premiums paid by the smallest firms are these manual premiums. The vast majority of all employers in the USA pay unmodified manual premiums, though these employers have relatively few employees and only account for a small fraction of all employment covered by workers' compensation.

If the manual premium exceeds a given amount, then premiums are "experience-rated." In this case, the manual premium is modified to reflect the firm's own past injury loss experience. In the USA, the premium of an experience-rated firm is a weighted average of the manual premium and the firm's actual loss experience, where the weight placed on actual loss experience grows with firm size. That is, the extent to which a firm's actual premium reflects its own injury losses depends on the size of the firm. Small experience-rated firms pay premiums that largely reflect the manual premiums. In contrast, large experience-rated firms pay premiums that largely reflect their own loss experience rather than the average loss experience. The weight placed on the firm's own loss experience is termed the "degree of experience-rating." In the economic theory described below, it plays an important role in generating incentives for firms to invest in safety.

The foregoing describes how premiums are set for firms purchasing insurance from private carriers or state funds. Firms that self-insure bear all of the costs of workers' compensation benefits directly, resembling full experience-rating. However, simulations by Victor (1982) have shown that fully experience-rated premiums can provide stronger incentives for safety than self-insurance.

With respect to benefits, all state laws require nearly 100 percent coverage of medical expenses and some minimum cash benefits related to lost earnings for those out of work longer than the state-specific waiting period (2–7 days). Whether as compensation for lost earnings from temporary or permanent injury, or to survivors in the event of death, cash benefits are generally paid weekly and, subject to a minimum and maximum, are usually two-thirds of the workers' weekly pre-injury earnings. If the injury lasts longer than a period known as the retroactive period, the worker is also paid benefits for the waiting period.

3.2 Economic Theory of Workers' Compensation — Workers' Incentives

Economic theory predicts that the characteristics of the workers' compensation system affect the behavior of workers and employers in ways that alter observed injury and claim incidence, duration, and costs. Collectively, the impact of insurance on injury outcomes is termed "moral hazard," illustrated by the following models of worker and firm behavior.

Consider a stylized model of a worker's decisions in the presence of workers' compensation, where at the beginning of the period, a worker allocates effort to safety prevention (and "claim classification" if injured) at the beginning of the period, given workers' compensation benefit B and wage W. An occupational injury occurs with probability p. If there is no injury (with probability $1 - p$) then the worker receives a wage, W. If an injury occurs, it is one of two types: either it is a medical only injury which receives no compensation benefits (that is, receives no lost wage reimbursement), or it is a temporary total

(TT) injury which receives a period benefit of B. Whether or not the injury is classified as medical only or TT is subject to numerous random influences which can be influenced to some extent by the worker's efforts.

The worker can lower the likelihood of an injury by devoting effort, e, to accident prevention activities (adhering to safety protocol, wearing safety goggles, being attentive to the task at hand rather than day-dreaming, etc.). So the likelihood of an injury is:

$$\text{injury probability} = p(e) \quad \text{where } \partial p/\partial e < 0, \quad \partial^2 p/\partial e^2 > 0, \qquad (3.1)$$

that is, the worker's safety efforts are subject to diminishing returns. This assumes that the worker perceives some injury risk and is aware that his behavior affects that risk.

Similarly, the worker can also influence whether a claim is classified as medical only or temporary total by putting in additional effort, once an injury has occurred. Denote this classification effort by f, which may consist of claiming the injury is more severe than it is (strains and sprains are difficult to monitor as to their true level of severity, for example), or being more diligent in filing the claim, or finding a particularly sympathetic doctor, etc. More f effort increases the likelihood of receiving temporary total compensation given that an injury has occurred:

$$\text{likelihood of a TT claim} = \pi(f) \quad \text{where } \partial \pi/\partial f > 0;\ \partial^2 \pi/\partial f^2 < 0. \qquad (3.2)$$

The cost (in utility terms) of providing effort either to prevent the accident, e, or once the accident has occurred, putting in the effort, f, to get it classified as a TT compensable injury is given as:

$$\begin{aligned}&\text{Utility equivalent costs}\\ &\quad = C(e,f);\ \partial C/\partial i > 0,\ \partial^2 C/\partial i^2 > 0 \quad \text{for } i = e, f. \qquad (3.3)\end{aligned}$$

The cross derivative, $\partial^2 C/\partial e \partial f$, is indeterminate a priori. This cross-derivative indicates whether there are economies of scope between the effort to reduce accidents and the effort to have an accident classified as a TT claim, should an accident occur. That is, if that classification effort, f, decreases the marginal costs of safety efforts then $\partial^2 C/\partial e \partial f < 0$, and there will be economies of scope. In Equations (3.6a)–(3.6d), we assume that if there are economies of scope, they are not large, so that $p'\pi'[V - M] - C_{ef} \leq 0$.

Given these assumptions, the worker chooses safety effort, e, and classification effort, f, to maximize expected utility:

$$\begin{aligned} EU = {} & (1 - p(e))U(W) \\ & + p(e)\{(1 - \pi(f))M(0) + \pi(f)V(B)\} - C(e, f), \end{aligned} \tag{3.4}$$

where $U(.)$, $V(.)$, and $M(.)$ are the state-dependent utility values for income received when there is no injury, a TT injury, or a medical only injury, respectively. Maximization with respect to e and f yields the following first-order conditions (suppressing arguments where there is no ambiguity, and letting $\partial p/\partial e \equiv p'$; $\partial C/\partial e \equiv C_e$, etc.):

$$\begin{aligned} p'[(1 - \pi(f))M + \pi(f)V - U] - C_e = 0 \\ p\pi'[V - M] - C_f = 0. \end{aligned} \tag{3.5}$$

Differentiating these first-order conditions and solving for changes in effort given exogenous shifts in wages and benefits, yields the following results:

$$\frac{\partial e}{\partial W} = \frac{(p\pi''\tau - C_{ff})p'U'}{\Delta_1} > 0 \tag{3.6a}$$

$$\frac{\partial f}{\partial W} = \frac{(-p'\pi'\tau + C_{ef})p'U'}{\Delta_1} \gtrless 0$$

$$\text{(but will be} < 0 \quad \text{if } \partial^2 C/\partial e\, \partial f \geq 0) \tag{3.6b}$$

$$\frac{\partial e}{\partial B} = \frac{(p\pi''\tau - C_{ff})(-p'\pi V') + (p'\pi'\tau - C_{ef})(p\pi' V')}{\Delta_1} \gtrless 0$$

$$\text{(but will be} < 0 \quad \text{if } \partial^2 C/\partial e\, \partial f \geq 0) \tag{3.6c}$$

$$\frac{\partial f}{\partial B} = \frac{(p'\pi'\tau - C_{ef})(-p'\pi V') + (p''\mathcal{L} - C_{ee})(-p\pi' V')}{\Delta_1} \gtrless 0$$

$$\text{(but will be} < 0 \quad \text{if } \partial^2 C/\partial e\, \partial f \geq 0). \tag{3.6d}$$

The results assume that $\tau \equiv V(B) - M(0) > 0$ (more income is better: given that an injury has occurred, a worker would rather have the injury classified as a TT than a medical only claim), and that workers would prefer wage income for certain over a lottery between TT benefits and medical only benefits under a workers' compensation claim: $\mathcal{L} \equiv \pi(f)V(B) + (1 - \pi(f))M(0) - U(W) < 0$. These two inequalities are required for there to be interior solutions to the first-order conditions in Equations (3.5). While the firm is required by law to inform an employee of his or her workers' compensation benefits once an injury has occurred, and while the firm is required to prominently post information at the workplace on these benefits in most states, if workers don't read such postings or are unaware of workers' compensation benefits, the assumptions above may not hold ex ante as our model assumes. The determinant of the Hessian, Δ_1, will be positive by the second-order conditions for maximization.

This example illustrates how workers' compensation affects both true safety incentives and incentives to report or classify injuries. Kniesner and Leeth (1989) and Butler and Worrall (1991) establish the empirical importance of making this distinction between true safety incentives and reporting incentives under workers' compensation. The opportunity costs of being out-of-work on a workers' compensation claim are forgone wages not reimbursed by workers' compensation benefits, that is, roughly $W - B$ (wages less benefits). As indicated by the model, as wages go up (Equation (3.6a)) or benefits go down (Equation (3.6c)), assuming $\partial^2 C/\partial e\, \partial f \geq 0$), the worker makes greater accident prevention effort, e, resulting (on average) in fewer accidents. The real safety effect of benefits is reflected in e-type effort.

Both wages and benefits not only affect safety efforts, e, but also claim classification efforts (i.e., claims-reporting effort), f. In particular, assuming $\partial^2 C/\partial e\, \partial f \geq 0$, the higher are benefits or the lower are wages, the greater will be the effort to classify the claim as more severe (i.e., f increases so that the claim is more likely to be classified as a TT rather than a medical only claim in the model).

"Moral hazard" is an old insurance term to indicate incentive responses generated by insurance coverage, or changes in insurance coverage. This model illustrates that as insurance benefits increase, that is as B increases, there are changes in risk-bearing moral hazard response (the effort to prevent an injury, e, falls) as well as claims-reporting moral hazard (the effort to get your claim classified as more severe, f, rises). In this simple example, the claims-reporting moral hazard is simply the greater incentive to have the claim classified as a longer duration, TT claim instead of a medical only claim. However, the result holds in more complex models of worker behavior under workers' compensation insurance: as benefits rise, lowering the opportunity cost of being a claimant, workers have an incentive to stay out of work (in claimant status) longer on any given type of claim. That is, an increase in benefits not only increases the workers' willingness to file a claim, it increases the willingness to stay in claimant status longer.

3.3 Economic Theory of Workers' Compensation — Firms' Incentives

3.3.1 Experience-Rated Workers' Compensation Insurance Premiums

As discussed above, the premiums paid by firms for workers' compensation insurance coverage are a weighted average of their own workers' compensation payouts (with weight α) and the manual rates in their risk category (with weight $(1 - \alpha)$). When $\alpha = 1$, the firm is fully experience-rated and their insurance premium is essentially equal to their paid insurance benefits. When $\alpha = 0$ the firm is not experience-rated, so its insurance costs are simply the manual rate for the firm's risk group, regardless of the firm's own safety outcomes.

The firm's paid benefits consist of medical costs paid under both medical only claims and temporary total (TT) claims, D, and additional lost wage benefits, B, received only by TT claimants. Hence, benefits per injured worker are $\Pi(t)B + D$, where Π is the fraction of TT claims among all injured workers.

The firm tries to decrease the relative number of TT claims through effort, t. By reducing the fraction of all injuries that are TT, total benefit payouts are reduced. Firm's efforts to reduce TT claims are subject to diminishing returns, so that $\partial\Pi/\partial t < 0$ and $\partial^2\Pi/\partial t^2 > 0$. One type of reporting moral hazard incentive for the firm under experience rating is to deny an injury's TT claimant status (so workers' compensation premiums will go down).

$P(s)$ is the fraction of the workforce with an injury (either a medical only or a TT injury), a likelihood influenced by the firm's safety efforts, s, and subject to diminishing returns: $\partial P/\partial s < 0$ and $\partial^2 P/\partial\, s^2 > 0$. Hence the number of injured workers is $P(s)$ multiplied by N, and paid total workers' compensation benefits is $P(s)N[\Pi(t)B + D]$. A simplified model of insurance premiums paid by the firm under workers' compensation would be:

$$\text{WC Insurance premium} = \alpha P(s)N[\Pi(t)B + D] + (1-\alpha)FN \tag{3.7}$$

where F is the per worker manual rate for the firm's risk class.

The firm's real safety effort function is given by upper case $P(s)$, as it relates to the same safety outcomes as the worker's efforts to reduce an accident, given as a lower case $p(e)$ function: where s is firm's effort and e is worker's effort. Similarly, the firm's effort to prevent an injury from being classified as a TT claim is given as $\Pi(t)$, analogous to the worker's lower case function $\pi(f)$. The firm's s effort works on the same likelihood as the worker's e effort; the firm's t effort, as the worker's f effort. However, as we shall see, their incentives to influence any given outcome work in opposite directions as wages and benefits rise.

3.3.2 Profit Maximizing with Experience-Rated Workers' Compensation

The (risk-neutral) firm's problem is to maximize profits with respect to safety, s, and reporting efforts, t, given its production function, wage and insurance costs, and a safety and classification of claims cost function, $Z(s,t)$ (with properties $\partial Z/\partial s > 0, \partial Z/\partial t > 0, \partial^2 Z/\partial s^2 > 0, \partial^2 Z/\partial t^2 > 0$, and $\partial^2 Z/\partial t\partial s \equiv Z_{st}$, which is uncertain as to sign and magnitude):

$$\begin{aligned}\text{Profits} = {} & g((1-P(s))N) - W(1-P(s))N - \alpha P(s)N[\Pi(t)B + D] \\ & -(1-\alpha)FN - Z(s,t),\end{aligned} \tag{3.8}$$

where $g(.)$ is a concave production function and the firm's product price has been normalized to 1. Maximization with respect to s and t yields the following first-order conditions (suppressing arguments and letting $\partial P/\partial s \equiv P'$; $\partial Z/\partial s \equiv Z_s$, etc.):

$$\begin{aligned} -g'P'N + WP'N - \alpha P'N[\Pi B + D] - Z_s = 0 \\ -\alpha P\ N\ \Pi' B - Z_t = 0. \end{aligned} \tag{3.9}$$

Differentiating these first-order conditions and solving for changes in effort given exogenous shifts in wages, benefits, and the degree of experience rating we have the following results:

$$\frac{\partial s}{\partial W} = \frac{-P'N\Psi_{\mathrm{tt}}}{\Delta_2} < 0, \tag{3.10a}$$

where $\Psi_{\mathrm{tt}} \equiv -\alpha\ P\ N\ \Pi''B - Z_{\mathrm{tt}}$ is negative from the model assumptions and the determinant of the Hessian, Δ_2, is positive from the second-order conditions. Note this is the opposite of the worker's incentive: as W increases, the opportunity cost of being on a claim by the worker goes up, and so the worker tries to prevent injuries through increasing the worker's accident prevention efforts. The firm, on the other hand, sees payroll costs increasing (relative to the worker being on a workers' compensation claim), so that the opportunity cost of providing employment has risen and the firm has an incentive to reallocate some resources away from accident prevention efforts. As wages increase, accident prevention incentives of the worker and firm diverge (compare Equation (3.6a) with Equation (3.10a)).

The effect of an increase in the wage rate on classification efforts is unclear:

$$\frac{\partial t}{\partial W} = \frac{(-P'N)(\alpha P'N\pi'B + Z_{st})}{\Delta_2} \lesseqgtr 0 \tag{3.10b}$$

as the denominator is positive (by the second-order conditions), but the numerator is indeterminate in sign. The numerator will be positive, for example, if Z_{st} is non-negative or relatively small in magnitude (though Z_{st} will be negative if there are economies of scope in the provision safety and classification efforts). In that case, as wages rise, the firm's incentive to prevent the filing of TT claims increases as the cost of indemnity claims increases with the wage, and the number of TT claims will tend to fall, shown in (Equation (3.10b)). (Equation (3.6b)) indicates a similar outcome: higher wage makes working more attractive to the worker, and unless there are economies of scope between accident prevention efforts and claim classification efforts, this will reduce workers' efforts to have their claim classified as TT, and the number of TT claims will tend to fall on this account as well.

The effects of benefits and the degree of experience rating on firm's efforts are indeterminate without making any further assumptions:

$$\frac{\partial s}{\partial B} = \frac{\Psi_{tt}\,\alpha P' N \Pi + (\alpha P' N \Pi' B + Z_{st})(\alpha\ P\ N\ \Pi')}{\Delta_2} \lessgtr 0, \qquad (3.10c)$$

$$\frac{\partial t}{\partial B} = \frac{(\alpha P' N \Pi' B + Z_{st})(\alpha P' N \Pi) + \Psi_{SS}\,\alpha P N \Pi'}{\Delta_2} \lessgtr 0, \qquad (3.10d)$$

$$\frac{\partial s}{\partial \alpha} = \frac{\Psi_{tt} P' N [\Pi B + D] + (\alpha P' N \Pi' B + Z_{st})(P N \Pi' B)}{\Delta_2} \lessgtr 0, \qquad (3.10e)$$

$$\frac{\partial t}{\partial \alpha} = \frac{(\alpha P' N \Pi' B + Z_{st})(P' N [\Pi B + D]) + \Psi_{SS}(P N \Pi' B)}{\Delta_2} \lessgtr 0, \qquad (3.10f)$$

where, $\Psi_{SS} \equiv g''(P')^2 N^2 - g' P'' N + W P'' N - P'' \alpha N[\Pi B + D] - Z_{SS}$ is negative by the second-order conditions, and again $\Psi_{\rm tt} \equiv -\alpha P N \Pi'' B - Z_{tt}$ is negative from the model assumptions. The determinant of the Hessian, Δ_2, will be positive by the second-order conditions.

Nonetheless, none of these effects are definitely signed because of the indeterminacy of the sign and magnitude of $\alpha P' N \Pi' B + Z_{st}$: the left-hand side term is positive and the right-hand side term of cross-partial derivatives of the cost function will be negative if there are economies of scope in effort provision by the firm.

The $\alpha P' N \Pi' B + Z_{st}$ effect represents the interaction between the firm's reporting effects, t, and their safety prevention efforts, s — directly through the cross-derivative of the effort cost function, $Z(s,t)$, but also indirectly through the product of the safety response effect ($P' < 0$) and the classification effects ($\Pi' < 0$) in the $\alpha P' N \Pi' B$ term. We assume that these interaction effects are collectively small for the firm (say, $\alpha P' N \Pi' \approx -Z_{st}$) and dominated by the other terms in the expressions. If so, the effects of benefits and changes in the degree of experience rating have their intuitive effects:

$$\frac{\partial s}{\partial B} = \frac{\Psi_{tt}\,\alpha P' N \Pi}{\Delta_2} > 0, \tag{3.11a}$$

$$\frac{\partial t}{\partial B} = \frac{\Psi_{SS}\,\alpha P N \Pi'}{\Delta_2} > 0, \tag{3.11b}$$

$$\frac{\partial s}{\partial \alpha} = \frac{\Psi_{tt} P' N \left[\Pi B + D\right]}{\Delta_2} > 0, \tag{3.11c}$$

$$\frac{\partial t}{\partial \alpha} = \frac{\Psi_{SS}\, P N \Pi' B}{\Delta_2} > 0. \tag{3.11d}$$

Increases in lost wage reimbursement to employees under workers' compensation, B, increases both the firm's efforts to improve the real level of safety, s, and to reduce the proportion of TT claims through classification efforts, t. Again these incentives are opposite to those of the worker because benefit payments that lower workers' opportunity cost of being on a claim increase the firms' insurance costs under workers' compensation (compare Equations (3.6c) and (3.11a)). If the firm is not experience-rated (so the degree of experience rating is zero, $\alpha = 0$), then the benefit effects on effort in Equations (3.11a) and (3.11b) are zero. Note while the classification effects of Equations (3.6d) (workers) and Equations (3.11b) (firms) have the same sign, the efforts are working in opposite directions: an increase in workers' f effort increases the likelihood of TT classification, while an increase in the firm's t reduces the likelihood of TT classification.

The experience-rating effects in Equations (3.11c) and (3.11d) also work in the expected direction. The degree of experience rating, α, reflects the relative importance of firm's efforts on firm's costs: when $\alpha = 0$, and there is no experience rating, the cost of workers' compensation premiums become FN, fixed regardless of the safety or classification efforts of the firm. As α increases, so does the link between the firm's safety and classification efforts, and the firm's cost of insurance. Hence, efforts to prevent accidents (Equations (3.11c)) and efforts to have the proportion of accidents be medical only claims (Equation (3.11d)) increase.

3.4 Summary of Incentives under Workers' Compensation

There are offsetting incentive effects that influence the true level of safety. More generous benefits weaken workers' incentives to self-protect (take care on the job and take care while recuperating from an injury), resulting in an increase in the incidence and severity of resulting injuries. Conversely, more generous benefits may increase incentives for firms to invest in safety, as these more generous benefits are passed along to firms in the form of higher premiums. However, this firm incentive depends on the extent that premiums are tied to a firm's own loss experience. If a firm simply pays a manual premium that is not tied to its own loss experience, then higher workers' compensation benefits provide no additional incentive to avoid injuries (of course, other factors will provide this incentive). This is because the firm cannot lower its premium by investing in extra safety. However, the higher the degree of experience rating, the greater is the incentive for the firm to invest in safety to reduce its premiums.

Therefore, economic theory is uncertain about the impact of workers' compensation on the true level of safety. While it weakens workers' incentives to avoid injury and to recuperate, it may strengthen the incentives of firms to invest in safety.

Workers' compensation may also alter incentives for reporting injuries without changing the true level of safety (through workers' efforts f and firms' efforts t). Like the true safety incentives, the reporting incentives work in opposite directions for workers and for firms. Specifically, more generous benefits may increase workers' incentives to report off-the-job injuries as occurring on-the-job, to report injuries that don't exist, and to exaggerate the severity of injuries. Both changes in the true safety level, and changes in the propensity to file claims for any given level of safety, increase the reported incidence and severity of injuries in terms of lost weeks of employment.

Conversely, more generous benefits may cause firms to resist filing claims for injuries that have occurred. They may also cause firms to place injured workers on light duty either to avoid workers' compensation claims or to bring workers back to work earlier. These firm incentives decrease the reported incidence and severity of injuries. Like the firm's true safety effect, the extent to which firms resist filing claims and bring workers back to work earlier will depend on the extent to which premiums are experience-rated. Butler and Worrall (1991) termed these reporting effects "claims-reporting moral hazard."

3.5 Workers' Compensation Insurance — Empirical Evidence

3.5.1 Injury Benefits and Claim Incidence

A number of empirical studies have measured the effect of workers' compensation on the incidence of occupational injuries and claims.[3] These studies analyzed both workers' compensation claims data and injury rate data. The studies generally find that an increase in benefits is associated with an increase in the incidence of claims and injuries. This supports the contention that the incentive effects for workers tend to dominate those for firms.

A group of studies have analyzed the injury rate data collected by the Bureau of Labor Statistics (BLS).[4] These data distinguish between injuries that involve lost workdays and injuries that have no lost workdays. The results from studies using these data generally showed that higher benefits increased the rate of lost-workday injuries more than the rate of injuries without lost workdays. Chelius (1982) found that a 10 percent increase in benefits increased the rate of lost workday cases by 1.2 percent, while increasing the rate of cases not involving lost workdays by only 0.7 percent (an effect that was not statistically significant). Ruser (1985) found that a 10 percent increase in benefits increased the rate of lost workday cases between 1.2 and 3.1 percent depending on the model specification, while the increase for all cases (including those without lost workdays) was between 0.6 and 2.8 percent.

Similar results have been found in workers' compensation claims data. For example, in aggregate data for 35 states in the 1970s, Butler and Worrall (1983) found that a 10 percent increase in benefits was associated with a 4 percent increase in claims (a claims rate/benefit

[3] Many of these studies are reviewed in Worrall and Butler (1986) and Smith (1992).

[4] These data measure the annual number of new injury cases per 100 full-time workers.

elasticity of 0.4). Butler and Worall (1988) fit generalized loss distributions on 11 manual rate risk categories (roughly, occupations) for 38 states using detailed workers' compensation losses (insured firm-level data), for two years, and find a benefit elasticity of 0.47. Similarly, Chelius and Kavanaugh (1988) examined a particular case where workers' compensation benefits were reduced. They found that this resulted in a decline in workers' compensation claims.

Butler (1983) using aggregate claims for 15 industries over a 32-year period in South Carolina, estimates benefit to claim frequency elasticities generally from 0.13 to 1.1. Butler et al. (1997) use a difference-in-difference estimator for workers' compensation claims from a single large inter-state employer, identifying the benefit elasticity from four large increases in the workers' compensation maximum weekly benefit for different states, and one state with a large decrease in the workers' compensation maximum benefit. The logistic, difference-in-difference estimators implied claims rate/benefit elasticities from 0.4 to 1.1, even for the state with the large decrease in the maximum benefits (in that state, claim rates want down substantially following the decrease — suggesting a symmetric impact of benefit changes).

Beyond these overall results, further research has focused on a variety of issues, including whether experience-rating strengthens firms' incentives for safety and whether it is possible to separate reporting and true safety incentives.

Evidence tends to support the hypothesis that experience-rating strengthens firms' economic incentives for safety, but not all research is conclusive. Among the stronger results, Ruser (1985, 1991) showed that higher benefits raised injury rates less in larger, more experience-rated firms. Ruser (1991) analyzed BLS injury rates for separate establishments (individual businesses or plants). Depending on the statistical model, he found that a 10 percent increase in weekly benefits increased injury rates by 3.8–7.7 percent in establishments with fewer than 100 employees. In contrast, this benefit increase raised injury rates by at most 1.8 percent in establishments with more than 500 workers. Ruser interpreted this as evidence that experience rating in larger firms strengthens incentives for safety, counterbalancing the worker disincentive effect.

Utilizing the same basic methodology as Ruser (1985), Worrall and Butler (1988) also found confirming evidence that "experience-rating matters" in workers' compensation data from the state of South Carolina. They obtained stronger evidence for permanent partial disabilities than for temporary total disabilities.[5]

Besides experience rating, another mechanism that strengthens the link between a firm's workers' compensation benefits paid to its workers and its insurance costs is the use of large deductibles in insurance policies. The larger the deductible, the greater the incentive to reduce costs: if deductibles exceed expected workers' compensation benefits consumed by the workers, the "insurance" would be essentially the same as being fully experience-rated or self-insured. Durbin and Butler (1998) regress state-level fatal workplace injury rates on the introduction of large deductible insurance policies during the 1980s and find a significance decrease in fatalities associated with larger deductibles, and also significant decreases in fatal workplace injury rates associated with increases in experience rating coverage among firms.

However, not all researchers are convinced that experience-rating provides strong employer incentives for safety. In two separate studies, Chelius and Smith (1983, 1993) failed to find empirical support for the hypothesized incentive effect of experience-rating. They provided a variety of explanations for their negative results. Among these, they noted that the premium adjustments due to experience rating tend to be relatively small and, owing to the way that premiums are calculated, premium savings from safety appear several years in the future. Also, since the formula for calculating experience-rating is complicated, they questioned whether employers understand the financial incentives.

A potential shortcoming of the studies of Ruser and others is that they analyze outcomes such as injury or claims incidence that are influenced both by changes in safety and in reporting[6]. Critics of the experience-rating hypothesis argue that, even when supported by evidence, it may result not from reductions in true safety, but merely from firm's activities to reduce reported injuries. In an interesting study of

[5] The result for temporary total disabilities is not statistically significant.
[6] Durbin and Butler's (1998) analysis of fatal injury rates avoids this criticism.

experience-rating, Thomason and Pozzebon (2002) analyzed the data they collected from 450 firms in the Canadian province of Quebec. These data provided information directly about firms' activities both to improve the safety and health conditions at the workplace and to manage claims.[7] Claims management involves activities that can reduce the cost of injury and disease to the firm without necessarily affecting workplace health and safety. These include activities taken to speed the injured worker's return to work and activities to challenge the worker's claim for benefits. In general, the statistical analysis of Thomason and Pozzebon supported the hypothesis that experience-rating causes employers both to improve workplace health and safety and to engage in more aggressive claims management.

Attempts to address empirically the distinction between true safety incentives and claims-reporting moral hazard have also focused on differences in possible reporting of different types of injuries. One strain of the literature focuses on the impact of workers' compensation on fatalities as compared to non-fatal injuries. The rationale is that it is more difficult to misreport a work-related fatality as opposed to a non-fatal injury. In contrast to the bulk of the literature on non-fatal injuries, Moore and Viscusi (1990) and Ruser (1993), using data from a census of death certificates and the BLS injury data respectively, found that death rates generally declined with benefits. They inferred that this reflected a true safety effect, whereas there was no claims-reporting effect.

Other studies have started from the hypothesis that worker-generated claims-reporting moral hazard is more likely to occur for injuries that are hard to diagnose or whose work-relatedness is hard to establish. The implication is that more generous benefits increase the frequency of hard-to-diagnose injuries such as back sprains, relative to

[7] Variables to measure health and safety practices included: presence of in-house safety personnel, hiring of a safety consultant, safety duties performed by safety personnel, presence of a worker employer safety committee and the number of meetings held by that committee, safety training time provided to employees, and firm expenditures on personal protective equipment. Claims management practices included: presence of in-house claims management personnel or the hiring of a claims management consultant, the extent to which the firm has placed disabled workers on temporary assignments, and the number of compensation claims resulting in a formal dispute.

easier-to-diagnose injuries like fractures and cuts. An implicit assumption needed to generate such a result empirically is that the effects of workers' compensation on true safety incentives and on firm-generated claims-reporting moral hazard are the same for all types of injuries.

The evidence on the effect of higher benefits on the relative frequency of hard-to-diagnose injuries is not unanimous, but tends to support the hypothesis of worker-generated claims-reporting moral hazard. In three manufacturing plants, Robertson and Keeve (1983) found that a higher maximum benefit increased the number of subjectively verified injuries and claims such as back sprains and pain, but there was no effect of higher benefits on lacerations and fractures. In contrast, Welland (1986), studying workers' compensation claims data for six states in 1976, found that more generous weekly benefits decreased the proportions of sprains and contusions, but increased the proportions of easily diagnosed amputations, burns, fractures, and scratches. In state level workers' compensation claims data, Butler et al. (1996) found that higher benefits increased the relative frequency of sprains and strains and decreased the frequency of cuts. Anomalously, they also found that the proportion of fractures increased with benefits. Finally, in BLS injury rate data, Ruser (1998) found that more generous benefits increased hard-to-diagnose back sprains and carpal tunnel syndrome relative to cuts and fractures.

Three studies examine the issue of the timing of reported injuries. Smith (1990) argued that workers' compensation creates incentives for workers to report hard-to-diagnose off-the-job injuries as having occurred on the job. Since there are more off-the-job hours preceding Mondays and the days after long weekends (referred to collectively as "Mondays") than before regular Tuesdays through Fridays, more off-the-job injuries occur prior to Mondays. Then, hard-to-diagnose injuries will be disproportionately reported on Mondays compared to other regular workdays. Consistent with this hypothesis, Smith showed in workers' compensation claims data that a greater proportion of sprains and strains relative to fractures and cuts were reported earlier in the work week and work shift than at other work times.

Contrary to Smith, two other studies failed to find a Monday effect. Using Minnesota workers' compensation claims data, Card and

McCall (1996) showed that workers who were less likely to have health insurance coverage were not more likely to report injuries on Monday compared to other days, as would be expected if workers use workers' compensation to provide health insurance. They also showed that the wage replacement rate did not exert an independent effect on the probability of Monday injuries. Finally, Ruser (1998) found that higher benefits increased the reporting of all injuries on Mondays, but did not raise the probability of a Monday-reported back sprain relative to a Monday-reported cut or fracture.

In sum, the empirical literature tends to support the hypothesis that more generous workers' compensation benefits induce more reported injuries and claims, particularly for injuries that are hard to diagnose or relate to the workplace. Workers' incentives tend to dominate those of firms. However, experience-rating does tend to enhance firms' incentives both to invest in safety and to engage in claims management to reduce claims.

3.5.2 Injury Benefits and Claim Duration

In addition to the rather voluminous literature on the impact of workers' compensation on injury and claims incidence, there is also a literature on claim duration, measured generally in terms of the number of lost workdays. This literature tends to find that higher benefits are associated with longer time away from work (termed an "out-of-work spell"). Perhaps the earliest of these studies is Butler and Worrall (1985), who examined variations in the duration of low back claims with respect to socio-economic characteristics and the wage replacement ratio. They found a benefits/duration elasticity of about 0.4: for each 10 percent increase in benefits, the duration of the claim increased by about 4 percent. Worrall and Butler (1985) find benefits/duration elasticities of about the same magnitude.

Meyer et al. (1995) analyzed the impact of an increase in the maximum income benefit in two states, Kentucky and Michigan. They found that a 10 percent increase in benefits was associated with a 3–4 percent increase in the duration of an out-of-work spell, similar to Butler and Worrall (1985). Other researchers have found larger impacts, including

Gardner (1991) who found that a 10 percent increase in benefits in Connecticut led to a nearly 10 percent increase in duration and Krueger (1990), who found that this benefit increase resulted in an over 16 percent increase in duration in Minnesota. Johnson and Ondrich (1990) also estimate relatively high benefits/duration elasticities, around 1.1 and 1.2.

It is important to note that even if workers' incentives to remain off the job dominate firms' incentives to bring workers back to work, it is not a priori certain that more generous benefits will result in longer average durations. Smith (1992), Meyer et al. (1995), Butler et al. (1997, footnote 1), and Ruser and Pergamit (2004) argued that there are two effects. On the one hand, more generous benefits provide incentives for workers to remain off the job longer (termed "malingering"). On the other hand, as indicated previously, more generous benefits may induce workers to report more injuries and claims. If these injuries tend to be minor, then more generous benefits result in a larger number of short duration injuries and claims. This "compositional" effect would tend to reduce average durations. Ruser and Pergamit (2004) found some evidence to support this effect. Counter to most results, they found that a 10 percent increase in the weekly benefit lowered the duration of all workers' compensation claims by over 5 percent. However, when claims of 7 days or longer were examined, there was no effect of higher benefits, suggesting that "compositional" effects were weaker and malingering effects stronger for more severe injuries.

As with injury and claims incidence, there is evidence that experience-rating strengthens firms' incentives to shorten out-of-work durations. Chelius and Kavanaugh (1988) found that the severity of injuries declined in a particular college after that institution switched to self-insurance. In a broader set of Minnesota data, Krueger (1990) found that the duration of temporary total spells was about 10 percent shorter in self-insured firms than in privately insured firms. Krueger did note, however, that this result might arise not only because self-insured firms have greater incentives to bring workers back to work, but also because the group of firms that self-insure might have injuries that are less severe than privately insured firms, even after controlling for observable covariates.

Benefits also seem to have different effects on duration depending on the type of injury. Dionne and St-Michel (1991) found in Quebec data that higher benefits increased the duration of hard-to-diagnose back injury cases, but had no effect on durations of objectively determined contusions, amputations, and fractures.

3.5.3 Extensions

The foregoing indicates that higher benefits are associated with longer duration workers' compensation claims. This would suggest that an appropriate strategy for inducing workers to return to work earlier would be to reduce benefits. This would be an erroneous strategy, as there is evidence that earlier return to work is associated with a higher probability of subsequent out-of-work spells. Butler et al. (1995) reported that Ontario workers receiving higher benefits were less likely to experience multiple absences from work, perhaps because longer initial absences from work resulted in more complete recoveries.

In addition to income benefits, a variety of other administrative and legal factors may influence the incidence and duration of claims and injuries. Filing for workers' compensation benefits is costly, while the success of a claim is uncertain. Any administrative or legal change that increases the cost or reduces the expected benefit of a claim may result in fewer claims and greater caretaking by workers. In response to rapidly increasing medical costs, a variety of USA states passed laws in the 1990s that restricted the worker's choice of doctor, reduced the compensability of certain injury cases, increased fraud detection, and capped legal fees. Despite the intent of these laws, Ruser and Pergamit (2004) were not able to detect a reduction in injuries or claims after the laws' enactments.

4

Government Intervention and Workplace Safety

Government can affect workplace safety and health in different ways. First, it can provide the rules under which workers' compensation insurance operates. The incentive effects of workers' compensation were just discussed. Second, government can directly intervene in workplace safety through the establishment and enforcement of safety standards and through the provision of safety information. This latter channel of influence, emphasizing the USA case, will be the focus of this section.

4.1 Occupational Safety and Health Act

Prior to 1970, US workplace safety and health was the purview of state and local government authorities. In that year, the USA Congress passed the Occupational Safety and Health Act, which established the USA Occupational Safety and Health Administration (OSHA) to regulate workplace safety in most of the private sector.[1] OSHA was given the task of establishing and enforcing workplace safety and health

[1] In 1969, the US Congress passed the Mine Safety and Health Act to cover the mining sector. Other groups of workers outside the jurisdiction of OSHA include transportation workers, many public sector employees, and the self-employed.

standards and to provide compliance training. Under the law, each state was given the opportunity to opt out of OSHA purview if the state could demonstrate that its own safety and health program was at least as stringent as OSHA. Twenty-one states maintain their own programs for the private sector, including some larger states such as California and Michigan.

OSHA conducts different types of inspections and levies fines on firms not in compliance with safety law. Large establishments are randomly inspected in high-risk industries, while other inspections focus on establishments identified through referrals, complaints, or the occurrence of a fatality or catastrophe. In Fiscal Year 2004 (October 2003 through September 2004) OSHA conducted 39,167 inspections, of which 55 percent (21,576) were random inspections targeted toward high hazard industries. OSHA also provides outreach, education, and compliance assistance, including free workplace consultations. It reported 31,334 consultations in Fiscal Year 2004. State partner agencies conducted an additional 57,866 inspections, of which 59 percent (34,116) were targeted at high hazard industries. While these inspection and consultation numbers appear high, it is important to remember that the US had well over 7 million private sector establishments during this time period.

4.2 Economic Theory of Workplace Safety and Health Regulation

To model the impact of OSHA inspection activity on firms' safety effort, denote an expected OSHA fines function (to the firm) as dependent upon OSHA activity γ and the firm's true level of safety, $P(s)$:

$$\textit{OSHA fines} = H(\gamma, P(s)), \tag{4.1}$$

where $\partial H/\partial\gamma > 0$, $H_P \equiv \partial H/\partial P > 0$, $H_{\gamma P} \equiv \partial^2 H/\partial\gamma\partial P > 0$. The expected fine increases with both the level of OSHA inspection activity and the probability of an injury in the firm. The second cross-partial derivative is essential in calculating the firm's response to OSHA efforts: saying that this cross-partial derivative is positive is equivalent to claiming either that total safety fines increase in more risky workplaces (if γ represents the size of the fine per violation) or that inspection frequency increases in more risky workplaces for any given level of fine (if γ represents the likelihood of a safety inspection).

Adding Equation (4.1) to the firm's costs (and suppressing the firm's classification efforts, t, in the profit function), we have:

$$\begin{aligned} \mathit{Profits}(s) = & \, g((1 - P(s))N) - W(1 - P(s))N - \alpha\, P(s)N[\Pi B + D] \\ & - (1 - \alpha)FN - Z(s) - H(\gamma, P(s)). \end{aligned} \quad (4.2)$$

Maximizing firm's profits with respect to the firm's safety efforts, s, yields the following first-order conditions:

$$-g'\, P'N + W\, P'N - \alpha\, P'N[\Pi B + D] - Z_S - H_P P' = 0. \quad (4.3)$$

Solving this for the effect of OSHA activity on firm's safety efforts we get:

$$\begin{aligned} \frac{\partial s}{\partial \gamma} & = \frac{P' H_{P\gamma}}{\Lambda} > 0, \quad (4.4) \\ \Lambda & = g''(P'N)^2 - g'P''N + WP''N - P''\alpha N[\Pi B + D] \\ & \quad - Z_{SS} - H_{PP}(P')^2 - H_P P'' \end{aligned}$$

where the denominator on the right-hand side of Equation (4.4) is negative by the second-order conditions, and the numerator is also negative as $P' < 0, H_{P\gamma} > 0$. Thus, increased OSHA inspection activity raises the level of firm safety effort. Again, two things drive the firm's safety response to OSHA activities: (1) expected safety fines lower firm's profits, and/or (2) OSHA activity is greater (whether defined in terms of monetary fines per violations, or the number of safety inspections) where expected injury risk is greater ($H_{P\gamma} > 0$). However, an important criticism of OSHA is that the fines are too low and inspections too infrequent to generate any significant response by firms (the analysis of Kniesner and Leeth, 2004, on mine inspections, discussed below, deals directly with these objections).

4.3 Empirical Studies of the Effectiveness of OSHA

As researchers generally believe that OSHA activities do increase the expected costs of workplace injuries (i.e., believe that $H_{P\gamma} > 0$), a number of studies have sought to determine whether OSHA is effective in reducing occupational injuries and illness. Most of these studies, summarized below, concluded that OSHA has had little or no effect. A small number of studies came to a different conclusion, though even these researchers concluded that OSHA's effectiveness at injury reduction has declined over time.

OSHA research focuses on several different avenues through which OSHA inspections might reduce injuries: the number of inspections, the number of violations of safety standards for which an inspected firm is cited, and the size of monetary fines assessed for violations. These studies also distinguish between general and specific deterrence effects. General deterrence effects arise as a firm reacts to changes in the general safety inspection environment: the probability that an inspection will occur, the average number of violations detected, and the average fine per violation. Specific deterrence effects arise when a specific establishment is inspected. Specific deterrence is about changes in injury rates for a specific firm when that firm is inspected and a violation is detected or fine assessed.

4.4 Estimating OSHA Inspection Effects in the Presence of Endogenous Inspections

In principle, general deterrence effects can be detected by relating injury rates (at the level of the individual establishment or for a group of establishments) to aggregate measures of inspections, violations, and fines. Similarly, in principle, specific deterrence effects can be detected by examining the injury rates of specific establishments that are and are not inspected, cited for violations or fined. The difficulty is that inspections are made where there are perceived problems, either in high-risk industries or in establishments that have had problems. Thus, a simple correlation between inspection activities and injury rates will tend to show that inspections raise injuries. Sophisticated statistical techniques must be employed to account for the jointly endogenous nature of injuries and inspections.

An early approach to addressing the problem of joint endogeneity of injuries and inspections was implemented by Smith (1979) and subsequently by McCaffrey (1983) and Ruser and Smith (1991). In order to estimate specific deterrence effects, instead of comparing inspected firms to uninspected firms, Smith compared firms inspected early in a given year to those inspected late in the year. He reasoned that since both groups of firms were inspected in the year, they would tend to exhibit similarities in whatever unmeasured characteristics were causing them to be inspected. But, the injury rate of late inspectees will largely reflect the forces at work prior to the inspection, while the injury rate of early inspectees should also reflect the impact of the inspection. Thus, the late inspectees form a comparison group against which a specific inspection effect can be estimated.

A second approach to addressing the joint endogeneity of injuries and inspections is to estimate a system of equations in which the two variables are jointly and simultaneously determined. Bartel and Thomas (1985) employed such an approach. Using two-stage least squares, they estimated three equations on pooled cross-section, time series data in which the unit of observation was a three-digit SIC-manufacturing industry in each of the years 1974–1978. The three endogenous variables were an injury rate (the number of lost workdays per worker), industry non-compliance with OSHA standards (penalties per inspection divided by employees per firm), and OSHA inspection activity (inspections per worker). The system was identified by the differing sets of variables that the researchers included in each of the equations.

Gray and Scholz (1993) introduce yet another approach to addressing the endogeneity problem. Previous work by Scholz and Gray (1990) found that the occurrence of an inspection in a manufacturing plant depended heavily on the plant's injury level but not on the percent change in injuries. Thus, Gray and Scholz (1993) proposed to estimate changes in injuries as a function of present and lagged inspections. However, the researchers noted that there are several shortcomings to this approach, which could bias the estimated impact of inspections. These included unobserved plant heterogeneity, serial correlation in the dependent variable, and the fact that current levels of enforcement might depend on the recent past history of injuries in the plant. The last problem could lead to falsely estimating that inspections reduced injuries. To understand this, imagine that injuries in a plant were abnormally high in a particular year and that once OSHA learned of this, it inspected the plant in the following year. Since injury rates tend to regress to the mean (Ruser, 1995), injuries in the year of inspection will tend to be lower than in the previous year, even in the absence of the OSHA inspection. However, the statistical approach of regressing injury change on inspection activity may falsely attribute the decline to the OSHA inspection, when the true cause is regression to the mean.

Gray and Scholz (1993) employed a sophisticated econometric approach of Chamberlain (1982, 1984) to address the three potential sources of bias in their initial model. As described in their article, the Chamberlain method provides a systematic procedure for dealing with these three biases and others in panel data. Further, the Chamberlain method provides a test of one source of bias in the presence of another source of bias. The Chamberlain method involves regressing each year of the dependent variable on all years of the independent variables (past, present, and future). The result is a large matrix of regression coefficients. The goal of the method is to find the theoretically relevant model that best explains the coefficient matrix. The approach is to specify a number of nested models (simpler to more complex) that impose different restrictions on the coefficient matrix. A Chamberlain χ^2 test indicates whether an added parameter or set of parameters in a more complex model improves the model's explanatory power over the simpler model.

Using the Chamberlain method, Gray and Scholz found that a simple model relating only contemporaneous inspection activity to changes in injuries was rejected in favor of a model that included lagged inspection effects. They also found evidence supporting the inclusion of plant fixed effects. However, conditional on including plant fixed effects in the regression, there was no evidence of serial correlation in the dependent variables and no evidence of endogeneity of inspections with respect to injuries.

4.5 Empirical Evidence

As stated earlier, the bulk of the earlier empirical investigations could find little or no effect of OSHA. In an analysis of OSHA's general deterrence effect in manufacturing from 1973 to 1983, Viscusi (1986) concluded that OSHA's influence was quite modest, reducing injuries by about 1.5–3.6 percent or 1–2 injuries per 1,000 workers. In a series of articles, Smith (1979), McCaffrey (1983), and Ruser and Smith (1991) measured the effect of OSHA on inspected firms (measuring a specific deterrence effect) and reached similar conclusions. For example, Ruser and Smith (1991, p. 234) concluded that "there is little evidence to suggest that OSHA inspections in the early 1980s were effective in reducing the lost-workday injury rate".

The apparently poor performance of OSHA can be explained in at least three ways. First, given the relatively small number of inspections, the low size of monetary fines and the relatively large number of potential establishments to be inspected, the probability of an inspection with a large fine is low. Employers may not find it cost-effective to respond to the weak incentives stemming from a low probability event, and hence, they may remain in non-compliance with standards. Second, some researchers believe that the OSH Act is flawed, because it emphasizes standards for capital equipment when most injuries are caused by the complex interaction of labor, equipment and the workplace environment. Bartel and Thomas (1985) found support for this second hypothesis, showing that while OSHA inspections had a significant effect in reducing violations, this did not translate into a lower injury rate. Third, the apparently poor performance of OSHA may reflect the fact that firms generally maintain safe work environments, perhaps in response to other economic incentives. Thus, OSHA inspections would not be expected to cause much improvement in safety.

It may be, however, that the previously cited studies were simply not sensitive enough to detect OSHA's effects on injuries. More recent studies, using more sophisticated methodology and better data, provide stronger evidence of OSHA inspection effectiveness. These studies focused on OSHA effectiveness once an inspector has detected a violation. Analyzing manufacturing plants from 1979 to 1985, Gray and Scholz (1993) found that inspections imposing penalties induced a 22 percent decline in injuries and a 20 percent decline in lost workdays in inspected plants in the three years following inspections.

However, the inspection effects reported by Gray and Scholz (1993) declined over time. Utilizing a consistent methodology over several time periods, Gray and Mendeloff (2005) found that the impact of an OSHA penalty inspection declined from 19 percent in 1979–1985 to 11 percent in 1987–1991 and a statistically insignificant 1 percent in 1992–1998. The researchers had a difficult time explaining this decline. They speculate that "increases in workers' compensation costs in the 1980s may have led employers to pay more attention to safety hazards, reducing the incremental incentives to improve safety provided by OSHA inspections." (Gray and Mendeloff, 2002, p. 19). This explanation is consistent with the third explanation provided above.

Since the Mine Safety and Health Administration (MSHA) does for mines what OSHA does for non-mining firms, and since MSHA provides for relatively frequent inspections and relatively large fines, it provides a natural comparison for OSHA efforts in a specific industry (namely mining) with well-defined technologies and safety issues. Kniesner and Leeth (2004) exploit this comparison, merging several data sets on mining activity to analyze the cost-effectiveness of enforcement activities using a panel data set with mine-specific information. They find, using the most favorable specifications, that the costs of inspection activity far exceed the benefits, suggesting that the health of miners could be vastly improved by reallocating some of the MSHA budget toward heart disease screening and more on-site defibrillators. To the extent that MSHA and OSHA activity have similar consequences, this suggests that OSHA activity would NOT be more cost-effective simply by increasing the number of fines or frequency of inspections.

4.6 Effectiveness of Safety Regulation in Canada

While the previous section has reviewed the evidence regarding the US safety enforcement regime, there is also some limited evidence from Canada. There appear to be few or no studies of other countries. Lanoie (1992b) examined the effect of the creation of Quebec's Commission de la Santé et Sécurité du Travail (CSST), by comparing industry injury rates after the creation of CSST (1981–1987) with those before CSST (1974–1980). He found significant declines in all accidents in four industries after CSST was created: construction (−4.7%), manufacturing of transport equipment (−5%), manufacturing of electrical products (−1.1%), and miscellaneous manufacturing industries (−3.9%). Further, Lanoie (1992a) found some evidence that the frequency of injuries (but not the severity) declined with inspections. Lanoie estimated that a 1 percent increase in the inspection rate was associated with a long-run decrease in the frequency of accidents of 0.21–0.30 percent. However, Lanoie (1992a) found no effect of certain innovative CSST policies such as compulsory prevention programs, the right of workers to refuse hazardous tasks, and the creation of joint employer-worker safety committees.[2] In Alberta Canada over 1987–1992, Auld et al. (2001) found little evidence that Alberta Occupational Health and Safety reduced the risk of accident and injury on construction worksites. However, on-site safety inspections did reduce the probability of death in some construction sub-industries.

[2] A recent study provides an explanation why the policy of employee right to refuse hazardous work may have no effect. Harcourt and Harcourt (2000) reported that the right to refuse was restricted. Employees had to satisfy many conditions to qualify for protection from employer discipline after refusing work.

5

Other Economic Influences

The previous three sections of this monograph have discussed three areas of the economics of occupational safety and health that have received the most attention in the literature. Other economic influences affect occupational safety and health. These include economies of scale in the production of safety, short-run macroeconomic fluctuations in business conditions, and long-run trends.

5.1 Economies of Scale

The data clearly indicate that, holding everything else constant, larger establishments (businesses or plants) are safer. In part, this may reflect the incentives created by workers' compensation insurance pricing discussed previously. However, this also likely reflects economies of scale in the production of safety. Larger firms may have lower costs of producing safety and, therefore, mays be more likely to invest in safety. These lower costs come about in part because certain operations may cost the same regardless of the size of the business. Setting up a safety department to help meet regulatory mandates may have the same cost, regardless of whether a business has ten people or a thousand. Hence, it is more likely that the thousand person business will set up the safety department than will the ten person business.

Similarly, safety training is relatively the same cost, regardless of whether it is provided to ten people or one hundred. For this reason, the large business is more likely to offer that training.

5.2 Economic Cycles

Changes over time in injuries are associated with short-run macroeconomic fluctuations. Research has shown that workplace injuries tend to fluctuate with macroeconomic business cycles, rising with economic upturns and falling with downturns (Smith, 1973). Four sources have been identified for this relationship. First as businesses increase production during a business cycle upswing, they increase the use of overtime hours. This causes fatigue and lapses in judgment that result in increased injuries. Second, as the business upswing becomes better established, employers both recall workers who were previously laid-off and hire new workers. The previously laid-off workers will tend to be younger and less experienced, while newly hired workers will be unfamiliar with the employer's plant and equipment. Research has shown that less experienced workers tend to have higher injury rates so the increased use of them during an economic upturn will show up as an increase in the aggregate injury rate. Third, to meet increased demand for output, firms may also bring into service previously surplused equipment. This equipment will tend to be older and may be relatively unprotected by safety devices, or have less effective safety devices. Workers may also be less familiar with this equipment. For these reasons, higher injury rates may be associated with the use of surplused equipment as compared to equipment that is used on a daily basis. Finally, recalling the model above of reporting efforts versus real safety effects, there may be no change in the real level of safety over the business cycle, but a "moral hazard" response in that workers are less willing to report injuries when job opportunities are scarce and unemployment high (Boone and van Ours, 2006).

5.3 Long-Run Trends

Over the long run, it is clear that the rate of workplace injuries has tended to decline. This reflects at least three factors: growing wealth and income, the increased price of labor relative to capital, and technological progress.

Growing income leads to an increased demand for goods, including nicer cars, bigger houses, more leisure (less working time), better health, and greater safety on the job. Thus, as an economy grows and its population becomes wealthier, the demand for safety increases. This operates through the mechanism of compensating wage differentials described earlier. As workers become wealthier, they demand larger compensating wage differentials to bear the same amount of risk (Viscusi, 1978). Employers also see risk as becoming more expensive, so they invest in more safety equipment to reduce their wage costs. This shows up over time as reductions in injuries.

Over time, the wages that workers are paid have increased, even relative to inflation. Economists attribute this growing wage to increased worker productivity, arising from increases in the amount of human capital that workers have acquired from education and training, and from on-the-job training. Since the wage rate equates to worker productivity, the wage also indicates how much is lost due to production delays when a worker is injured. Wages are also positively related to costs associated with hiring and training a replacement worker when an injury reduces the specific human capital of a firm. Thus, growing wages tend to mean growing injury costs for employers. Firms will invest in additional safety in order to avoid these losses in firm specific human capital.

Technological progress in equipment and computer technology also has increased the productivity of capital equipment. In some industries, for example, auto manufacturing and mining, this has resulted in the heavier use of capital equipment in production. Fewer workers are needed to produce the same amount of output and the workers tend to be higher skilled machine operators who are less likely to be in high injury risk situations. For these reasons, the long-run substitution of capital for unskilled labor has resulted in a decline in injuries.

Finally, safety has improved through technological progress in its production. Like every other aspect of the production process, there is continual innovation in techniques for ensuring safety in the workplace.

6

Conclusions

While workplace injuries occur at random, the actions of employers, workers, and government can influence the incidence, severity and duration of injuries. Safety is jointly produced along with market products[1] (cars, electricity, haircuts, etc.). Like any good, the quantity of safety produced is subject to market supply and demand.

Employers, workers, and possibly government provide inputs into the safety production process. As more safety inputs are used in the production of safety, the quantity of safety produced increases, lowering the incidence, severity, and duration of injuries. Employers invest in safety inputs in the form of safety equipment, protective devices installed on equipment, worker safety training, monitoring of workplace conditions, safety incentive programs, and safety departments staffed by experts. Workers decide whether to work at a risky job, how much safety effort and attention to bring to the job, whether to use provided safety equipment, and whether to pay attention during safety training. Governments may directly provide safety inputs, for example, by

[1] For an early monograph on the production of safety, see Oi (1974).

giving safety information to workers and firms. Or, governments may influence the safety decisions made by workers and firms through safety standards or the mandate of partial wage reimbursement or experience rating under a workers' compensation insurance system.

As we have seen, many of the incentives that affect the inputs into the production of safety and that affect the true safety level, may also affect incentives for reporting injuries. That is, changes in reported injuries (that are captured in injury surveys or administrative data) may arise without any change in the underlying level of safety. For example, employers may have incentives to keep injured workers on the job so that they don't have to pay higher future workers' compensation insurance premiums. Some of the studies of data reviewed in this monograph describe efforts to separate reporting effects from true safety effects.

This monograph has discussed how economic incentives affect occupational safety decisions of workers and firms, and how government can influence those incentives. Workers and firms respond to the costs and benefits of workplace safety that are generated by workers' compensation insurance, government regulation, and the market.

Workers' compensation insurance, established by state law, creates safety incentives in firms to the extent that premiums are tied to the accident loss experience of those firms ("experience-rating"). But income benefits paid to workers can weaken workers' safety incentives by reducing the costs of injuries to workers. The empirical literature suggests that these adverse worker incentives tend to dominate firm safety incentives, so that more generous income benefits lead to more frequent and longer duration injuries and claims. However, it is possible that this is in part a reporting, rather than a true safety effect.

The evidence for the USA and Canada suggests that government safety inspections have not been very effective in improving workplace safety. Two explanations that have been given for this are that: (1) the low probability and size of fines create weak safety incentives, and (2) the safety standards are not effective in reducing injuries. However, it is also possible that firms are largely in compliance with safety standards owing to incentives generated by workers' compensation insurance and the market.

The market has an influence on workplace safety, even absent government intervention through regulation and the establishment of workers' compensation insurance. Economic theory suggests that workers who are knowledgeable about job risks demand wage premiums to work at riskier jobs (compensating wage differentials). In deciding whether to invest in safety, firms compare savings in wage premiums against the cost of extra safety. Workers decide whether to work at a particular job based on whether the wage–risk premium is sufficient to compensate for the risk on that job. Consistent with this theory, data from a variety of countries provide empirical evidence of compensating wage differentials.

Finally, other economic factors influence injury and claims variations across firms and over time. Everything else equal, larger firms tend to be safer than smaller ones. This is because larger firms can spread some relatively fixed safety costs over a larger number of workers ("economies of scale"). Injury rates tend to increase with upswings in the economy, as workers work more overtime (leading to fatigue), and as firms both hire less experienced, riskier workers and utilize obsolete equipment that might not have the most up-to-date safety devices. Over time, injury rates tend to decline reflecting the increasing cost of labor, substitution of capital for labor, improvements in safety technology, and higher incomes that raise the demand for safety.

References

Aldy, J. E. and W. K. Viscusi (2007), 'Age differences in the value statistical life: revealed preference evidence'. *Review of Environmental Economics and Policy* **1**(2), 241–260.

Auld, M. C., J. C. H. Emery, D. V. Gordon, and D. McClintock (2001), 'The efficacy of construction site safety inspections'. *Journal of Labor Economics* **19**(4), 900–921.

Bartel, A. P. and L. G. Thomas (1985), 'Direct and indirect effects of regulation: A new look at OSHA's impact'. *Journal of Law and Economics* **28**(1), 1–25.

Boone, J. and J. C. van Ours (2006), 'Are recessions good for workplace safety?'. *Journal of Health Economics* **25**, 1069–1093.

Butler, R. J. (1983), 'Wage and injury rate response to shifting levels of workers' compensation'. In: J. D. Worrall (ed.): *Safety and the Work Force: Incentives and Disincentives in Worker's Compensation*. Ithaca, NY: ILR Press.

Butler, R. J., D. L. Durbin, and N. M. Helvacian (1996), 'Increasing claims for soft tissue injuries in workers' compensation: Cost shifting and moral hazard'. *The Journal of Risk and Uncertainty* **13**(1), 73–87.

Butler, R. J., B. D. Gardner, and H. H. Gardner (1997), 'Workers' compensation costs when maximum benefits change'. *Journal of Risk and Uncertainty* **15**, 259–269.

Butler, R. J., W. G. Johnson, and M. L. Baldwin (1995), 'Managing work disability: Why first return to work is not a measure of success'. *Industrial and Labor Relations Review* **48**(3), 452–469.

Butler, R. J. and J. D. Worall (1988), 'Labor market theory and the distribution of workers' compensation losses'. In: P. S. Borba and D. Appel (eds.): *Workers' Compensation Insurance Pricing: Current Programs and Proposed Reforms*. Boston: Kluwer Academic Publishers, pp. 19–34.

Butler, R. J. and J. D. Worrall (1983), 'Workers' compensation: Benefit and injury claims rates in the seventies'. *The Review of Economics and Statistics* **65**(4), 580–589.

Butler, R. J. and J. D. Worrall (1985), 'Work injury compensation and the duration of nonwork spells'. *Economic Journal* **95**(375), 714–724.

Butler, R. J. and J. D. Worrall (1991), 'Claims reporting and risk bearing moral hazard in workers' compensation'. *The Journal of Risk and Insurance* **58**(2), 191–204.

Card, D. and B. P. McCall (1996), 'Is workers' compensation covering uninsured medical costs? Evidence from the 'Monday effect''. *Industrial and Labor Relations Review* **49**(4), 690–706.

Chamberlain, G. (1982), 'Multivariate regression models for panel data'. *Journal of Econometrics* **1**(18), 5–46.

Chamberlain, G. (1984), 'Panel data'. In: Z. Griliches and M. Intriligator (eds.): *Handbook of Econometrics* , vol. 2. Amsterdam: North Holland, pp. 1247–1318.

Chelius, J. R. (1982), 'The influence of worker's compensation on safety incentives'. *Industrial and Labor Relations Review* **35**(2), 235–242.

Chelius, J. R. and K. Kavanaugh (1988), 'Workers' compensation and the level of occupational injuries'. *The Journal of Risk and Insurance* **55**(2), 315–323.

Chelius, J. R. and R. S. Smith (1983), 'Experience-rating and injury prevention'. In: J. D. Worrall (ed.): *Safety and the Workforce*. Ithaca, NY: ILR Press, pp. 128–137.

Chelius, J. R. and R. S. Smith (1993), 'The impact of experience-rating on employer behavior: The case of Washington state'. In: D. Durbin and P. S. Borba (eds.): *Workers' Compensation Insurance: Claim Costs, Prices, and Regulation.* Boston: Kluwer Academic Publishers, pp. 293–306.

Dionne, G. and P. St-Michel (1991), 'Workers' compensation and moral hazard'. *The Review of Economics and Statistics* **73**(2), 236–244.

Dorman, P. (1996), *Markets and Mortality.* Cambridge: Cambridge University Press.

Dorman, P. and P. Hagstrom (1998), 'Wage compensation for dangerous work revisited'. *Industrial and Labor Relations Review* **52**(1), 116–135.

Durbin, D. and R. J. Butler (1998), 'Prevention of disability from work related sources'. In: T. Thomason, J. F. Burton, Jr., and D. Hyatt (eds.): *Disability in the Workplace: Prevention, Compensation and Cure.* IRRA, Madison, WI.

Gardner, J. A. (1991), *Benefit Increases and System Utilization: The Connecticut Experience.* Cambridge, MA: Workers' Compensation Research Institute.

Gegax, D., S. Gerking, and W. Schulze (1991), 'Perceived risk and the marginal value of safety'. *The Review of Economics and Statistics* **73**(4), 589–596.

Gray, W. B. and J. M. Mendeloff (2002), 'The declining effects of OSHA inspections on manufacturing injuries: 1979–1998'. National Bureau of Economic Research, Working Paper No. 9119.

Gray, W. B. and J. M. Mendeloff (2005), 'The declining effects of OSHA inspections on manufacturing injuries: 1979–1998'. *Industrial and Labor Relations Review* **58**(4), 571–587.

Gray, W. B. and J. T. Scholz (1993), 'Does regulatory enforcement work? A panel analysis of OSHA enforcement'. *Law and Society Review* **27**(1), 177–213.

Harcourt, M. and S. Harcourt (2000), 'When can an employee refuse unsafe work and expect to be protected from discipline? Evidence from Canada'. *Industrial and Labor Relations Review* **53**(4), 684–703.

Hersch, J. (1998), 'Compensating differentials for gender-specific injury risks'. *The American Economic Review* **88**(3), 598–607.

Hersch, J. and T. S. Pickton (1995), 'Risk-taking activities and heterogeneity of job-risk trade-offs'. *Journal of Risk and Uncertainty* **11**(3), 205–217.

Johnson, W. G. and J. Ondrich (1990), 'The duration of post-injury absences from work'. *Review of Economics and Statistics* **72**(4), 578–586.

Kniesner, T. J. and J. D. Leeth (1989), 'Separating the reporting effects from the injury rate effects of workers' compensation insurance: A hedonic simulation'. *Industrial and Labor Relations Review* **42**(2), 280–293.

Kniesner, T. J. and J. D. Leeth (1991), 'Compensating wage differentials for fatal injury risk in Australia, Japan, and the United States'. *Journal of Risk and Uncertainty* **4**(1), 75–90.

Kniesner, T. J. and J. D. Leeth (2004), 'Data mining mining data: MSHA enforcement efforts, underground coal mine safety, and new health policy implications'. *Journal of Risk and Uncertainty* **29**(2), 83–111.

Kniesner, T. J. and J. D. Leeth (2009), 'Hedonic wage equilibrium: Theory, evidence and policy'. *Foundations and Trends® in Microeconomics* **5**(4), 229–299.

Kniesner, T. J., W. K. Viscusi, and J. P. Ziliak (2006), 'Life-cycle consumption and the age-adjusted value of life'. *Contributions to Economic Analysis & Policy* **5**(1), Article 4.

Krueger, A. B. (1990), 'Workers' compensation insurance and the duration of workplace injuries'. Industrial Relations Section, Princeton University, Working Paper No. 261.

Lanoie, P. (1992a), 'The impact of occupational safety and health regulation on the risk of workplace accidents: Quebec: 1983–1987'. *The Journal of Human Resources* **27**(4), 643–660.

Lanoie, P. (1992b), 'Safety regulation and the risk of workplace accidents in Quebec'. *Southern Economic Journal* **58**(4), 950–965.

Leeth, J. D. and J. W. Ruser (2003), 'Compensating wage differentials for fatal and nonfatal injury risk by gender and race'. *The Journal of Risk and Uncertainty* **27**(3), 257–277.

Leigh, J. P. (1991), 'No evidence of compensating wages for occupational fatalities'. *Industrial Relations* **30**(3), 382–395.

Leigh, J. P. (1995), 'Compensating wages, value of a statistical life, and inter-industry differentials'. *Journal of Environmental Economics and Management* **28**(1), 83–97.

McCaffrey, D. (1983), 'An assessment of OSHA's recent effects on injury rates'. *The Journal of Human Resources* **18**(1), 131–146.

Meyer, B. D., W. K. Viscusi, and D. L. Durbin (1995), 'Workers' compensation and injury duration: Evidence from a natural experiment'. *The American Economic Review* **85**(3), 322–340.

Moore, M. J. and W. K. Viscusi (1990), *Compensation Mechanisms for Job Risks*. Princeton: Princeton University Press.

Oi, W. Y. (1974), 'On the economics of industrial safety'. *Law and Contemporary Problems* **38**(4), 669–699.

Pouliakas, K. and I. Thoedossiou (2010), 'An inquiry into the theory, causes and consequences of monitoring indicators of health and safety at work'. Discussion Paper no. 4734, IZA.

Robertson, L. S. and J. P. Keeve (1983), 'Worker injuries: The effects of workers' compensation and OSHA inspections'. *Journal of Health Politics, Policy and Law* **8**(3), 581–597.

Rosen, S. (1974), 'Hedonic prices and implicit markets: Product differentiation in pure competition'. *Journal of Political Economy* **82**(1), 34–55.

Rosen, S. (1988), 'The value of changes in life expectancy'. *Journal of Risk and Uncertainty* **1**(3), 285–304.

Ruser, J. W. (1985), 'Workers' compensation insurance, experience-rating, and occupational injuries'. *RAND Journal of Economics* **16**(4), 487–503.

Ruser, J. W. (1991), 'Workers' compensation and occupational injuries and illnesses'. *Journal of Labor Economics* **9**(4), 325–350.

Ruser, J. W. (1993), 'Workers' compensation and the distribution of occupational injuries'. *The Journal of Human Resources* **28**(3), 593–617.

Ruser, J. W. (1995), 'Self-correction versus persistence of establishment injury rates'. *The Journal of Risk and Insurance* **62**(1), 67–93.

Ruser, J. W. (1998), 'Does workers' compensation encourage hard to diagnose injuries?'. *The Journal of Risk and Insurance* **65**(1), 101–124.

Ruser, J. W. and M. R. Pergamit (2004), 'Workers' compensation reforms and benefit claiming'. Paper presented at the 3rd International Conference on Health Economics, Policy and Management, Athens, Greece.

Ruser, J. W. and R. S. Smith (1991), 'Reestimating OSHA's effects: Have the data changed?'. *The Journal of Human Resources* **26**(2), 212–235.

Scholz, J. T. and W. B. Gray (1990), 'OSHA enforcement and workplace injuries: A behavioral approach to risk assessment'. *Journal of Risk and Uncertainty* **3**(3), 283–305.

Smith, A. (1776), *An Inquiry into the Nature and Causes of the Wealth of Nations* (often cited simply as, *Wealth of Nations*). London, W. Strahan and T. Cadell.

Smith, R. S. (1973), 'Intertemporal changes in work injury rates'. In: *Proceedings of the Industrial Relations Research Association*, 25th Annual Meeting. pp. 167–174.

Smith, R. S. (1979), 'The impact of OSHA inspections on manufacturing establishments'. *The Journal of Human Resources* **14**(2), 145–170.

Smith, R. S. (1990), 'Mostly on Mondays: Is workers' compensation covering off-the-job injuries?'. In: P. S. Borba and D. Appel (eds.): *Benefits, Costs, and Cycles in Workers' Compensation.* Boston: Kluwer Academic Publishers, pp. 115–128.

Smith, R. S. (1992), 'Have OSHA and workers' compensation made the workplace safer?'. In: D. Lewin, O. S. Mitchell, and P. D. Sherer (eds.): *Research Frontiers in Industrial Relations and Human Resources.* Madison, WI: Industrial Relations Research Association, pp. 557–586.

Thomason, T. and S. Pozzebon (2002), 'Determinants of firm workplace health and safety and claims management practices'. *Industrial and Labor Relations Review* **55**(2), 286–307.

Victor, R. B. (1982), 'Workers' compensation and workplace safety: The nature of employer financial incentives'. Rand Corporation Report R-2979-ICJ.

Viscusi, W. K. (1978), 'Wealth effects and earnings premiums for job hazards'. *The Review of Economics and Statistics* **60**(3), 408–416.

Viscusi, W. K. (1983), *Risk by Choice: Regulating Health and Safety in the Workplace*. Cambridge: Harvard University. Press.

Viscusi, W. K. (1986), 'The impact of occupational safety and health regulation'. *The RAND Journal of Economics* **17**(4), 567–580.

Viscusi, W. K. and J. E. Aldy (2003), 'The value of a statistical life: A critical review of market estimates throughout the world'. *The Journal of Risk and Uncertainty* **27**(1), 5–76.

Viscusi, W. K. and J. Hersch (2001), 'Cigarette smokers as job risk takers'. *The Review of Economics and Statistics* **83**(2), 269–280.

Welland, D. A. (1986), 'Workers' compensation liability changes and the distribution of injury claims'. *The Journal of Risk and Insurance* **53**(4), 662–678.

Worrall, J. D. and R. J. Butler (1985), 'Benefits and claim duration'. In: J. D. Worrall and D. Appel (eds.): *Workers' Compensation Benefits: Adequacy, Equity, and Efficiency*. Ithaca, NY: ILR Press.

Worrall, J. D. and R. J. Butler (1986), 'Lessons from the workers' compensation program'. In: M. Berkowitz and M. Anne Hill (eds.): *Disability and the Labor Market: Economic Problems, Policies, and Programs*. Ithaca NY: ILR Press.

Worrall, J. D. and R. J. Butler (1988), 'Experience rating matters'. In: P. S. Borba and D. Appel (eds.): *Workers' Compensation Insurance Pricing: Current Programs and Proposed Reforms*. Boston: Kluwer Academic Publishers, pp. 81–94.

Lightning Source UK Ltd.
Milton Keynes UK
UKOW05f1212161014

240183UK00001B/92/P